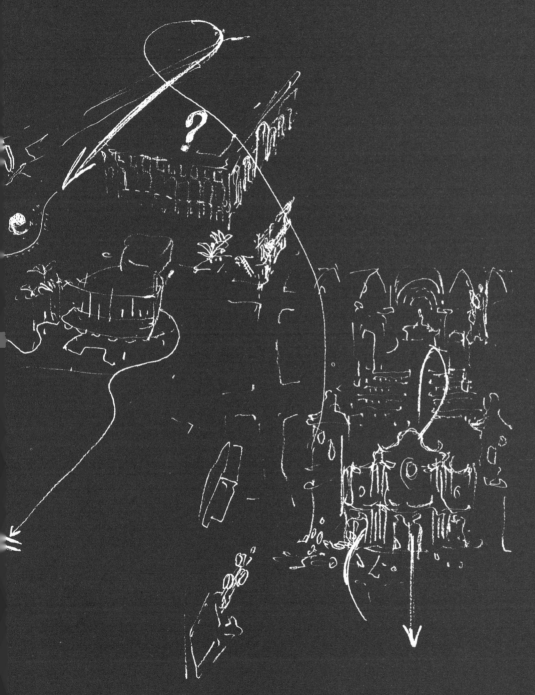

... fashion, workmanship.
... afraid of using the body, trusting to ...
penetrate or be penetrated by ...
... health, look! etc.; Nor ca...
... the body at the same time ...
... so different.

... body image, beautiful body ...
... in the country ... the meal ...
... down to show to them the ...
... that my body ... desir...
... desire others.

... pleasure of the body — exercise, ...
... the senses ... eating to el...
... coffee, starving to ...
... bad lifestyle. Not bei...
... other to be as one wants.
... with poison dangerous ...
... people. Experimenting ...
... how, conquering th...
... body. Being a wif...

Nigel Coates

JONATHAN GLANCEY

Nigel Coates

Body Buildings

and City Scapes

WATSON-GUPTILL
PUBLICATIONS
New York

First published in 1999 in the United States of America
by Watson-Guptill Publications, a division of
BPI Communications, Inc.,
1515 Broadway, New York, NY 10036

Library of Congress Catalog Card Number: 99-60302

ISBN 0-8230-1211-5

This book was conceived,
designed, and produced by
THE IVY PRESS LTD
2/3 St. Andrews Place
Lewes
East Sussex BN7 1UP

Art Director: Terry Jeavons
Design and page layout: Alan Osbahr
Commissioning Editor: Christine Davis
Editorial Director: Sophie Collins

Reproduction and printing in Hong Kong by
Hong Kong Graphic and Printing Ltd.

Contents

I never really thought of architecture as a good steady job so much as a pleasure, a way of life. My aim is to enrich the world around us, by working with it rather than against it. I want to get away from the grand vision, though it is up to architects to put forward ideas that perhaps haven't been thought of by others—whether clients or public. For me, architecture is the connective tissue between body and place. The idea and its translation into space should always be above matters of mere style. At Branson Coates our work aims to generate slippage, accentuate movement, and provoke a subtle turn-on. I like designing at all scales, from the chair through to the city itself. Architects had better get used to the fact that we're part of a much wider network that includes not only the building team but also curators, inventors, media mavericks, artists, graphic designers, writers, and filmmakers. The dawn of the millennium is an exciting time for our profession because we can truly talk of architecture that is not dependent on bricks and mortar; it could easily be hidden in the wider flow of the city, in a CD-ROM, or even a little book like this. **"**

Nigel Coates

NIGEL COATES ONCE BELIEVED he would never build. For a long time it seemed that he would remain a "paper architect," destined to generate controversy with provocative polemics and spirited drawings, and to spark enthusiasm in the minds of the students he taught at London's Architectural Association (AA), while real, live architecture eluded him. From the perspective of 1999, this seems quite remarkable. With the final touches being made to London's Millennium Dome "Body," and a spate of new projects either just opened or in the pipeline, Nigel Coates seems rarely out of the spotlight.

Nigel Coates founded Branson Coates Architecture (BCA), with Doug Branson, in 1985, on the back of the mid-1980s building boom that reshaped cities worldwide. Although based in London, it was in Tokyo—rapidly followed by Dublin, Glasgow, Amsterdam, and Istanbul—that Coates began to build. In fact, it wasn't until 1998 that Branson Coates completed its first building in Britain, an imaginative if restrained—even

gentle—extension to the Geffrye Museum in Shoreditch, East London. By this time, however, the practice was surfing on the back of a wave of international building projects and had become a major player on the architectural stage. Most remarkably of all, Coates proved that it was possible to connect popular taste with inventive new design. The extension to the Geffrye Museum was opened and praised by the Prince of Wales—a man for whom modern architecture has always been anathema, yet even here Coates's radical work held genuine appeal. Coates has often been described in the media as an *enfant terrible*, because his work is unfettered by tradition, and at times outlandish. By the time the Prince of Wales opened the Geffrye Museum extension, Coates had become all but an establishment figure. Inspired still, and unpredictable, but as a designer of national museums, no longer *terrible*.

Radical ideas

Coates's reputation for provocation was established when the first of the Tokyo bars and restaurants he designed took shape in the mid-1980s. These complex, sexy collage designs—which included

Caffè Bongo, Tokyo, 1986. The dramatic entrance (above), complete with aircraft wing and Corinthian column, leads to an interior where Piranesian Rome meets "Espresso Modern" (below).

The Bohemia Jazz Club, Tokyo (1986), an idealized, souped-up version of a beatnik hangout.

"Design needs to reflect the complex interaction of today's city. It should be knowing and reactive; it should encourage involvement and enquiry."

Noah chairs, 1988, initially designed by Coates for the Arca di Noè restaurant and subsequently produced by SCP, London.

the Metropole restaurant (1985), Caffè Bongo (1986), and Arca de Noè restaurant (1988)—reflected Coates's fascination with, and connection to, contemporary crosscurrents in music, fashion, the art world, and popular culture. Belonging to no school of design other than his own, he was free to explore radical new ideas that most of his fellow professionals found either gauche or absurd.

What surprised Coates's critics in the ensuing years was his being awarded important government commissions such as the *powerhouse::uk* exhibition (London, 1998), and the design of the British Expo pavilions at Lisbon (1998) and Hanover (2000). Even more baffling was the way in which BCA was so highly regarded by long-established and seemingly traditional British companies such as Christie's (master plan for auction room refurbishments, 1998) and Liberty (various departmental designs, 1992–96); indeed, this process had begun as far back as 1988 when BCA was commissioned to design a traveling exhibition for Alfred Dunhill to mark the family firm's centenary.

World Fish Restaurant in the Hotel Marittimo, Otaru, Japan (1989). Coates commissioned a group of artists to collaborate on the hotel (pictured above onsite).

"We live in a media- and information-saturated world of interactivity, yet the usual ambition of architecture is still limited to questions of form and function. We want it always to participate."

What went right? Although it might have seemed unlikely at the outset of the Thatcher-driven design boom of the 1980s, BCA not only matched and mirrored, but also stimulated, a growing desire for new kinds of imagery and a new culture. The significance of this only began to become clear after Mrs. Thatcher had been ousted from power and the "Cool Britannia" message of the Blair government, elected in 1997, was loudly broadcast.

Unit 10 and NATO

Coates had by this time come a long way from the AA days of "paper architecture," and very much farther from his roots in rural England. Born in Malvern, the son of a government scientist, Coates was educated at Nottingham University and the AA, graduating from there in 1979. He subsequently taught at the AA where, without courting it, he attracted controversy, notably when in 1983 two visiting professors, James Stirling and Edward Jones, dismissed the work of his diploma-year students. Neither of these two well-respected architects was willing to see in the eclectic, freewheeling, and fashionable work of Coates's Unit 10 (as his student group was

Katharine Hamnett menswear store, Tokyo, 1990: Branson Coates's third shop for the designer following the success of the London Sloane Street and Glasgow branches.

known) the seed of a fresh approach to their jealously guarded discipline. It was an approach that embraced the miasmic and sometimes dysfunctional life of modern cities and tried to weave architectural concerns through a web of urban excitement and urban schlock. The results were wild drawings that paid little or no lip-service to conventional architectural concerns with plan, section, and plumbing.

As a riposte to the damning judgment of Stirling and Jones, Coates established NATO (Narrative Architecture Today, also known as Nigel and the Others), a group of like-minded teachers, students, artists, architects, and hangers-on with an urban design agenda very much of its own. Coates's fellow conspirators were Catrina Beevor, Martin Benson, Peter Fleissig, Robert Mull, Christina Norton, Mark Prizeman, Melanie Sainsbury, and Carlos Villanueva. NATO published a punchy magazine of the same name, edited by Coates, with a circulation of 2,000.

Meanwhile, Coates had been recognized by the media and potential clients as an architect in touch with—and able to express—the design currents of the early 1980s; this meant being able to connect a funky traditionalism with a radical new sensibility. His own South Kensington apartment, published in *Harpers & Queen* in 1980, caught the mood perfectly; Peter York described it as a case of "Pasolini meets Palladio." This would lead in due course to Coates landing his first solid commission, the Metropole restaurant in Tokyo, and the formation of Branson Coates Architecture. More Japanese commissions followed, orchestrated by the entrepreneur Sy Chen, who had spotted Coates's potential early on. Chen set up the consultancy Creative Intelligence Associates, with the purpose of matching the designer with like-minded clients. The Japanese economy was booming, and Branson Coates was on a roll.

Multidisciplinary approach

What made Coates different, and hard for skeptical professionals to swallow, was his refusal to be pinned down as a designer. "When the practice was formed, our objective was to seed a multidisciplinary approach to architecture," he says. "Design, we felt, needed to reflect the complex interaction of today's city. It should be knowing and reactive; it should encourage involvement and

Airport runway meets pleasure palace: Taxim nightclub, Nightpark, Istanbul, 1991.

"Our work has become identified by its playful qualities, by accumulation and contradiction, by the overlaying of the extraordinary and the commonplace."

The Wall, Nishi Azabu, Tokyo (1990): a supposed chunk of Roman city wall behind a portion of cast-iron gasworks screen.

enquiry. Rather than being a sterile language of functional compartments, dressed in architectural clothes of this style or that, it should provide a living stage for cultural and social events." Coates sees the city as a living organism, which we need to respond to and learn from if we are to design effectively for the future. "We live in a media- and information-saturated world of interactivity, yet the usual ambition of architecture is still limited to questions of form and function. We want it always to participate." His desire to engage in as many aspects of city life as he can is expressed in a profusion of ways in the many restaurants, clubs, and shops that his practice has shaped over the past 15 years or so.

Despite his relatively newfound acceptance by the political, architectural, and educational establishments (he was appointed professor of Architectural Design at the Royal College of Art in 1995), Nigel Coates continues to revel in breaking the rules of taste and decorum. "From our new buildings to exhibitions and designs for furniture, our work has become identified by its playful qualities, by

Perfumery at Liberty, London, 1993. A silver-leaf ceiling adds height and grandeur to what was formerly a book department.

accumulation and contradiction, by the overlaying of the extraordinary and the commonplace, by artistic intervention, by a filmic handling of space. We enhance a world in which old hierarchies have been replaced by an interactive balance between owner and user, men and women, old and young, soft and hard, material and immaterial, real and virtual." His overriding vision is one of an architect whose job it is "to cut and paste . . . to match the programming of events to the programming of the terrain." He sees this new "soft planning" as a mixture of process-aware urbanism, architecture, design, and event devising.

Aesthetic risk-taking

Much of this was foreign to straitlaced architects, although much made sense. But it was Coates's increasingly successful attempts to realize these sentiments in three dimensions during the 1990s that, more than anything else, puzzled fellow architects. How could he please so many and such varied clients, be lauded by the Prince of Wales, Tony Blair's "New Labour" government, and the cultural avant-garde all at once? The answer is pretty simple: an open mind,

"We enhance a world in which old hierarchies have been replaced by an interactive balance between owner and user, men and women, old and young, real and virtual."

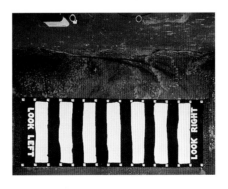

Black-and-white humor: zebra rug for V'soske Joyce, Ireland, 1990.

an ability to make unlikely cultural connections, and a great sense of humor (architects are not exactly famous for the last of these). Coates's warm, engaging, touchy-feely approach to life and the city has made him unlikely friends across the social and artistic spectrum and enabled him to evolve an architecture that has many centers and gives off many complex, even contradictory, messages. His work is not, however, postmodern in the formal architectural understanding of this much-maligned and often misrepresented term. It is, rather, contemporary; of now, and with now. There is rarely a sense of cool detachment in BCA's projects: the team, more or less, shares Coates's enthusiasm for living urban life to the full, while Coates himself claims that he learns just as much from his students at the Royal College as they do from him. Just as Nigel Coates is unable to look down on his students, so is he also unable to gaze down with a lofty architectural eye on the city—he wants to be, and is, a part of

it, on ground level. The practice's flights of fancy are tempered, although it might not always look like this, by this sense of genuine involvement. And this, presumably, is a feeling conveyed to Coates's wide range of clients. Coates has no interest in crusty debates over whether modern architecture is better or worse than traditional architecture; he simply lives his subject with an irrepressible energy.

Branson Coates takes aesthetic risks, and not all of its projects come off as smoothly as they might if the practice chose to be well-behaved and squeaky clean at all times. Yet the only real danger it faces is that of being taken up too wholeheartedly by established organizations and official bodies. The practice grew up in the 1980s with the bizarre radicalism of the Thatcher agenda; it has since been taken up by a government that has been busy consolidating the Thatcher revolution (at least that is how world history may well view this period of British history in years to come); now it needs to keep up a revolution within the revolution. But if Nigel Coates can't keep forever youthful and radical, what hope can there be for the rest of us?

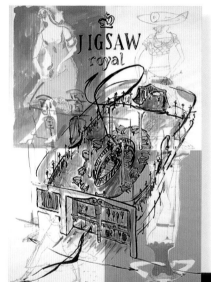

Jigsaw, Brompton Road, London, 1991: Branson Coates's third shop for the fashion chain. Sketch by Nigel Coates, background figures by Stewart Helm.

Jigsaw, Manchester, 1994 Bobbin-topped hanging rails evoke Manchester's industrial past.

Typically pneumatic: Pillow Bowls manufactured by Simon Moore, 1998.

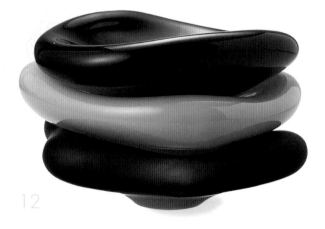

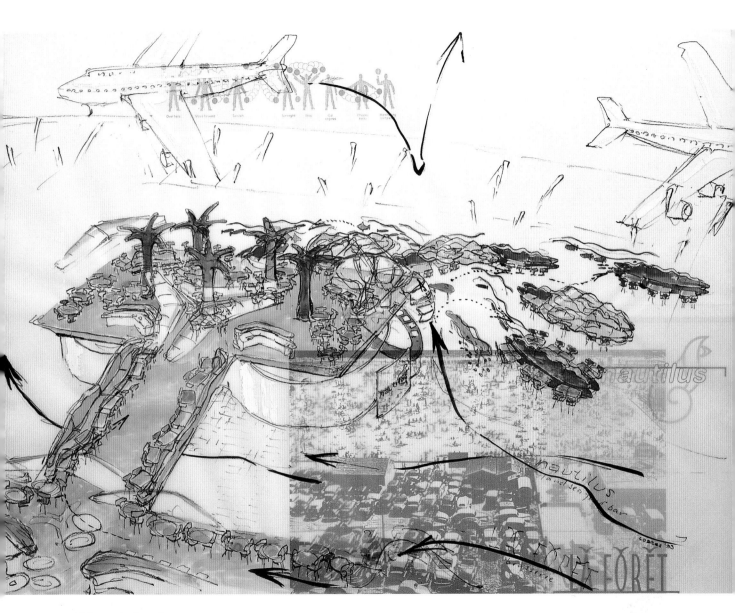

*"An exotic place where forest meets coral reef":
Nautilus and La Forêt restaurants, Schiphol Airport, Amsterdam, 1993. Design sketch by Nigel Coates.*

13

NIGEL COATES'S approach to urban design has never been less than provocative. It breaks the rules, seeing the city as a vibrant organism rather than a grid of geometric lines. It's about living, about meeting people, about accidental encounters, changes, risk-taking, sex. Most of all, it's about connecting people with the spaces they inhabit, whether indoors or out,

Ephemeral architecture: Ecstacity built of sand, shot for Vogue, *March 1993 (photo by Snowdon).*

or somewhere in between. Thus, a Coates drawing of a city project is a thing of energetic cross-currents, his city a live-wire traffic intersection where anything and everything promises to happen. Buildings, in Coates's view of the city, can never be separated from the spaces and places which they inhabit.

"It's about getting under the skin of the city," he says, "about going with the flow, seeing where it takes you, and then responding in appropriate ways. A healthy city, or a city you want to be in, is always changing; it's an organism, not a machine running on fixed lines. This sense of a city being alive informs both our response to the city as architects, and the individual buildings we design. These are very much about exploration, about making choices and feeling free rather than being constrained by strongly deterministic plans."

Commentaries to reference pictures by Nigel Coates.

Although seemingly irreverent, Coates's approach to urban design is actually a good deal less theoretical, less pie-in-the-sky—most of the time, anyway—than that of many more conventional architects, who often seem to be above the daily concerns of normal people. The ice-cold city plans conceived by architects over the past few decades—whether inspired by neo-classical Beaux-Arts formalism or an equally formal Modern Movement rationale—for the most part appear to have been conjured up with no sense of what a city is really like to live in. Of his own city schemes—such as the iconoclastic

ECSTACITY
Painting, 1992

Ecstacity at its most grandiose: this large-scale painting defines the spirit of Coates's experience-based attitude to the city, which he sees as a condition of continuous transformation.

ECSTACITY
Tri-Wonder billboards, 1992

Three visions of Ecstacity, rotating on slatted advertising billboards, suggest an infinite process of evolution for London. From left: Botticelli's Mars and Venus overlay their own energies onto the area between Trafalgar Square and St. Paul's; the body and a Tuscan landscape are grafted onto the same area; a head emerging from the "urban tide" gives rise to a series of vertical accents on the London landscape.

15

Ecstacity project shown at the Architectural Association in 1992, and *Eurofields*, a proposed redesign for London's King's Cross area exhibited at the Institute of Contemporary Arts in 1988—Coates says: "They're never meant to be overt provocations. In architecture, people assume that buildings and cities must have clarity, that you shouldn't get lost in them. But I see architecture and the city as setting up the conditions that will allow you to get lost, or to be surprised. Without the possibilities of experiencing that, a city becomes dull—you might as well live in Holland."

Ecstacity was an important point of departure for Coates. The project was his reaction to reading Jean Baudrillard's influential essay "The Ecstasy of Communication" (1987), in which the French philosopher announced: "We are no longer a part of the drama of alienation; we live in an ecstasy of communication." Baudrillard claimed that he found this "ecstasy" of communication "obscene." For Coates, however, the idea of a state of urban existence in which communications technology allows everyone to connect to everyone and everything else, was a purely positive one. For

Southwark, London, from the air displays the chaos of the medieval city (above). A tangle of discarded cable recalls the accidental way in which most cities grow up (below).

Coates, the "software city" was to be welcomed, as it could only enrich architecture by lacing it with another dimension. The solidity of architecture at the end of the twentieth century was now shot through with what Coates has called the "richly stimulating chaos" engendered by new forms of media and communications.

As Coates sees it, the perennial attempt made by architects to design wholly rational buildings, in a wholly rational city, is ultimately a sterile exercise. "The most delightful and the best-loved cities in the world are those that encourage us to

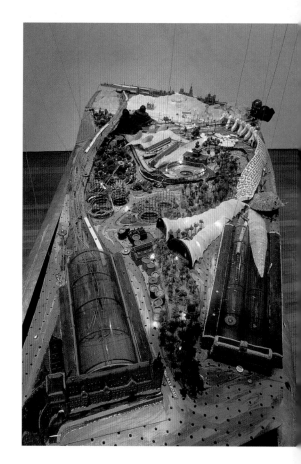

EUROFIELDS
Proposed redesign for King's Cross, 1988

Twisting and turning the city into and out of itself, this project aimed to rejuvenate a run-down area by reinvigorating the geographical link between London's King's Cross and St. Pancras rail stations.

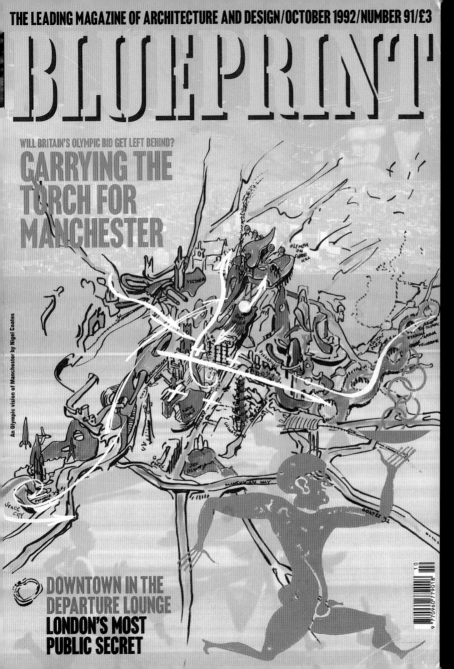

THE LEADING MAGAZINE OF ARCHITECTURE AND DESIGN/OCTOBER 1992/NUMBER 91/£3

BLUEPRINT

WILL BRITAIN'S OLYMPIC BID GET LEFT BEHIND?

CARRYING THE TORCH FOR MANCHESTER

An Olympic vision of Manchester by Nigel Coates

DOWNTOWN IN THE DEPARTURE LOUNGE
LONDON'S MOST PUBLIC SECRET

MANCHESTER
2000
Blueprint cover, October
1992

Blueprint magazine asked
Coates to explore
alternatives to the plans
being drawn up for
Manchester's millennial
Olympic Games bid. His
proposal entailed making
new connections between
places, buildings, and
cultures within the city in
the industrial heart of
England—the polar opposite
of the age-old idea of
"zoning," which divides
cities into role-specific
quarters. The plan includes
"virtual encounter bars," a
Space City, and a public
forum in the city center.

17

STAR BAR
Hotel Marittimo, Otaru,
Japan, 1989

**A tiny planetarium in which
to enjoy galactic cocktails.**

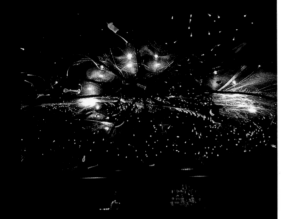

THE WALL
Nishi Azabu, Tokyo, 1990

**This commercial building
was designed by Branson
Coates to be a kind of
urban continuum, reflecting
and adding to the pulse of
the city.**

*Pissoir for passersby: artists
and designers were invited to
customize a London bus stop
for a 1996 exhibition; we
contributed a virtual urinal.*

*Buzzing past buildings on my
Ducati Monster: a good pace for
understanding the modern city.*

explore, to make
mental and physical
connections with
other places, secret
places, surprising
places, other people."
Coates's aim is to
connect the fabric of the city with the thrust and
pulse of modern life, to save a city from imploding
into a kind of (barely) living museum or a parody
of itself. "All our work, whatever its scale, emanates
from being in touch with contemporary issues,"
he says. "It's as much about the new electronic
age—the nightclub, the theme park, the
Internet—as about a city's history. Our work
deliberately bonds the viewer with the viewed,
the performers with the audience. We see the
nightclub as a key contemporary urban space—
but this doesn't preclude an understanding of
historical references, from classical to modern."

In an essay accompanying the *Ecstacity*
exhibition, Coates described how architects might
help plan cities in the future by learning to "go
with the flow" of urban life, learning to relax and
loosen themselves from the fetters of their formal
training and apparently ingrained desire for
neatness and order. He talked of a need for
architects to approach the city with a "cut-and-
paste" mentality, which would allow them to
"match the programming of events to the
programming of the terrain." They would thus

practice "a new 'soft'
planning, part process-
aware urbanism, part
architecture, part
design, part event-
devising." So, the
architect needs to take
a leaf out of the impresario's notebook—or the
conductor's, with the architect helping to fuse
together the sounds of the city (as well as the way
it feels, smells, and can be touched or otherwise
experienced). The architect needs to work out
natural, informal, or cleverly rigged ways of getting

19

Framing the city: a construction site provides an unknowing set-piece in which exchanges of time and scale stand side by side (above). Princess Diana window at Harrods: a spontaneous act of collective desire (below).

around and through the city, weaving together the disparate strands of the city without ever trying to force or dictate our experience of it.

As Coates points out, however, this is not something that architects can be expected to deal with overnight. "The way architects are trained, together with the kind of safe, middle-class backgrounds the majority of them come from, means that they are not the sort of people to take risks, nor are they likely to have experienced a city's life to the full. Architects still have a belief that they can somehow create perfect buildings for perfect people in a perfect world. At the Royal College of Art [where Coates is a professor of architecture], I encourage students to get out and about, away from their drawing boards and computer screens for much of the time. If not, they'll continue to see architecture as a discipline detached from the energy of urban life; they'll fail to see how architecture can never be as perfect as it seems in books or magazines, because a healthy city is one that exists in a state of constant change."

Coates wants the new generation of architects to loosen up, to see themselves as a part of everyday urban living rather than as latter-day Platonic guardians, in groovy glasses and black silk suits, who stand aloof and apart from it. Coates's approach to the design of cities represents a leap of the imagination away from sterile urban planning to a celebration of life at close quarters. "It's about letting the city be what it wants to be."

GAMMA-CITY
Air Gallery, London, 1987

Mounted by members of NATO, the Gamma-City represented "a focus model in which gamma buildings emitted rays of change across the city." It reflected NATO's concern to mesh public and private life.

ARKALBION
Architectural Association, London, 1984

This exhibition combined drawings with a huge model made from plaster, plastic, and "found" objects to convey a vision of the city in motion. The idea was to turn London's then-defunct County Hall into a living museum of urban processes, from health to politics, media to manufacturing.

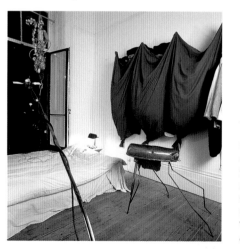

NATO BOUDOIR
Air Gallery, London, 1987

One of NATO's areas of experiment was to make new types of furniture. Objects by Mark Prizeman, Carlos Villanueva, Catrina Beevor, and Nigel Coates (who created the "Wombat Wardrobe") bring a gritty urban edge to the bedroom.

Living Bridges

LIVING BRIDGES was a magical show of model bridges drawn from across Europe and through history. Built to the same scale, they spanned a miniature River Thames flowing through the exhibition galleries of the Royal Academy of Arts, London, in the summer of 1996. The bridges were modeled on utopian concepts and built exemplars from medieval times to the present day. What they had in common was the fact that they were habitable bridges, lined with houses, shops, or, in one case, a giant parking garage. The exhibition also showed the winner and runners-up of a competition for the design of

Heroic backdrops: huge Old Master canvases casually propped against workshop walls.

a new "living bridge" to cross the Thames if a developer could be found to build it, and the planning permission given. As it turned out, developers were enthusiastic, but planners were not. Nevertheless, it was the most popular architecture exhibition the RA had ever mounted.

Designed by Branson Coates, the show recreated 22 "living bridges." These ranged from the phantasmagoric old London Bridge as it was in 1598 (when a German visitor counted no fewer than three heads of "traitors" stuck on poles from the bridge's perilous gables); through the exquisite Renaissance and classical bridges of Venice (Rialto), Florence (Vecchio), and Bath (Pulteney); to such determinedly modern visions as the bridge planned to house 1,000 cars over the Seine in Paris, designed by Konstantin Melnikov in 1925.

The models (made by Andrew Ingham & Associates) spanned a river of real water—stained a suitably urban dull brownish gray—that snaked through the gilded galleries of the RA. "We wanted to create a space of real fluidity and drama," says Coates. "We also had to make sense of a sequence of models that were unrelated, other than thematically, and were very disparate. We did this by giving the river a powerful backdrop of

The Living Bridges exhibition was designed (literally) to flow through the formal, classical enfilade of the Royal Academy, setting up a fresh dynamic. A backdrop of large-scale images was designed to give continuity and create a virtual cityscape.

Bridge visions: our entry for the Bankside Bridge competition, with Anish Kapoor, took the form of a silver blade or arrow across the Thames.

22

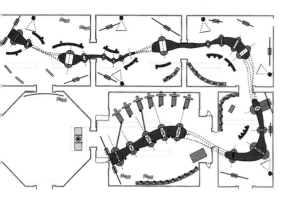

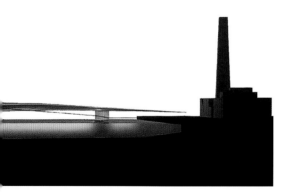

London Biennale, 2001:
a commission from
Perspectives *magazine*
resulted in this series
of proposed pavilions
on the River Thames.

23

giant photographs and other images propped on tiny easels, which were designed to make a kind of virtual cityscape with radically contrasting scales around them. From one point of view, the whole exhibition was a game of miniaturization and enlargement, designed to make people think of the relationship between monumental architecture and city streets." *Living Bridges* also brought together other characteristic Branson Coates themes: the baroque atmosphere of the RA rooms was achieved as much by reference to Coates's well-known fascination with nightclubs as by his vision of a city as a collage of fragments.

Branson Coates's own competition entry was seen by most observers as resembling a giant penis and testicles straddling the Thames. Coates denies this (with a grin), yet that is precisely what it looked like. "It was an exercise in plaiting together public spaces on either side of the river," he says. "The idea was for the cityscape to flow over the river, avoiding the feeling that the bridge itself was a kind of isolated monument or junction with just a single function. And that was the whole point of *Living Bridges*, to show how connections between places and spaces in a city are made, and demonstrate that these connecting devices can be as dramatic, likeable, and just as inhabitable as any other part of the city."

LIVING BRIDGES
Royal Academy, London, 1996

Giant visual backdrops (below and right) provided contrast with the scaled-down bridges that were the focus of this exhibition. Coates calls it "a game of miniaturization and enlargement, designed to make people think of the relationship between monumental architecture and city streets."

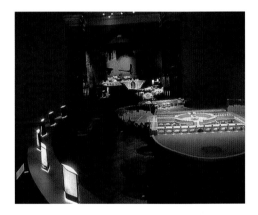

BRIDGE CITY
Competition entry, 1996

Branson Coates's entry to the Thames Water Habitable Bridge competition contained shops, cafés, and a hotel in a sequence of structures that interlocked at different levels. Many visitors, though, focused on the phallic nature of the design.

Bargo

OPENED IN 1996, Bargo is a big and bustling bar in the revived Merchant City quarter of Glasgow. This area has come alive in recent years, fueled by booze, bars, new design, and the Scottish city's concerted effort to pull itself out of the long depression that began when its heavy industries, particularly ship-building, all but sank in the 1960s. Glasgow has since reinvented itself to the extent that in 1999 it became Britain's City of Architecture and Design—a case of moving from ships to sushi in little more than a decade.

In a city famous for its heavy drinking, Bargo cuts-and-pastes together both the image and the reality of Glasgow life. Built inside the

Curious biomechanical props feature in Jeunet & Caro's film The City of Lost Children.

former Cheesemarket building, it speaks in what Coates terms the "packing-case language," reflecting in part the mercantile history of the area, and in part Glasgow's dockland and ship-building heritage. The imagery of the bar also draws on surreal sources such as Jeunet & Caro's film *The City of Lost Children*. "To get the right effect," says Coates, "we designed everything—the name of the bar, its graphics, signs, and furniture. By having complete control we were able to create a new kind of spatial freedom."

The effect is wholly theatrical. A new building slotted into an old one, it is by day a café, and by

1940s oil fields in the U.S. suggest a space that is both industrial and fanciful—qualities we were looking for in the design of Bargo.

night a bar with a nightclub underneath. Coates describes it as "a multilayered, three-story room that is like a theater in the round." The bar abounds in "eyecatchers," devices to draw the eye and encourage people to look across and through their surroundings. "Wherever you sit, you get

Bargo's "inner" and "outer" worlds are separated (in a revealing manner) by a screen at mezzanine level. A wing of giant mirrors bounces reflections from one side to the other.

BARGO
Glasgow, 1996

Bargo by night showing the sliding glass frontage.

Sometimes people themselves can form a space—I have often thought of nightclubs as the prototype for the city on the edge of the millennium.

Taxim combined luxury and good music with a Piranesian sense of scale.

Art arising from industry: one of Stewart Helm and Peter Fleissig's light-box pieces for our Jigsaw shop in Manchester.

glimpses of people in other parts of the bar," says Coates, "whether reflected in a giant mirror or caught through the mesh screen of the mezzanine. I see it as a kind of landscape, a pleasure garden rather than a one-take room." Rather than there being just one way up and through the bar, there are several. "The idea was to make it a fairly complex space so you get the feeling of there being possibilities here—of moving around, meeting people, flirting; the impression that there's always something else

happening just around the corner. Because of the building-within-a-building plan, you get the feeling that you're either outside looking in on the action inside, or the other way around. There's no fixed focus, no one way of experiencing the space."

The bar develops earlier ideas. "We started working on this approach in our design for the Taxim nightclub in Istanbul, in 1991. Here, people could walk around the dance floors and decide for themselves which part of the building they wanted to be in, rather than feeling forced to move through it in a specific way." Bargo itself, says Coates, is intended to be "moody and iridescent, somewhere that you feel is there to be explored, rather than a bar in which you settle on one stool or at one table and feel that's where you have to spend the rest of your evening. It's kind of cruisy, the sort of place where anything might happen—whether it does or doesn't."

BARGO
Glasgow, 1996

The bar draws on a number of sources—including the dockland and mercantile history of Glasgow—to create its theatrical effect. Old aluminum portholes are set into stainless-steel panels behind the bar, while overscaled beams and cratelike banquettes combine with the triple-height space to lend an industrial feel.

BARGO
Glasgow, 1996

Detail of the mezzanine screen (left); view showing Bargo's specially designed chairs and zinc-topped tables (right).

BARGO CHAIR
Omniate, 1996

Child's school chair meets oversized throne. Tough but cute, the Bargo Chair combines beechwood, steel, and metallized fabric.

BARGO
Glasgow, 1996

View from the upper bar, which is partially screened by an opalescent light-wall. The vast space of the former Cheesemarket serves as a café by day and a bar/nightclub by night.

The Power of Erotic Design

NIGEL COATES HAS ALWAYS seen the city as a highly charged and almost permanently erotic experience. He has tried to eroticize buildings, interiors, and furniture in ways that have been sensual, and also in ways that have been funny in a titillating, *double-entendre* kind of way. (His Genie Stool, a tall wooden stool complete with erect wooden phallus to hang onto or rub up against, is an example of the latter.) He was the obvious choice to give shape to the exhibition *The Power of Erotic Design,* held at the Design Museum, London, in 1997.

"This was a very difficult show to design," says Coates. "We didn't want it to be a place for people

The dark streets of London's Soho suggest illicit encounters.

with dirty minds to come and leer, nor did we want it to be chaste in a way that implied that the curators and designers had no interest, other than an academic one, in erotica. The objects chosen for the exhibition were also a very mixed bag: some were very beautiful and some downright unsubtle. So we had to think of a device that would hold the diverse elements together and be sexy in a low-key way. What we chose in the end was a pattern of screening exhibits from visitors, as if to stress the fact that the erotic element in design is often veiled from us; it's something that we either don't want to recognize, or can't recognize."

A further challenge for Branson Coates was how to combat the Design Museum's clinical, modernist whiteness. Dimmed lights, veils, and

Infinitely suggestive: veiled boudoir at Casa Devalle, Turin; interior by Carlo Mollino.

curvaceous forms helped the exhibition transcend its surroundings while propelling the very conventions of eroticism into a whole new dimension. The exhibition plan itself took the form of a sinuous maze that enticed the visitor into seemingly secret

THE POWER OF
EROTIC DESIGN
Design Museum, London
1997

Designing this exhibition was
a challenge to Branson
Coates, who wanted the
overall *ambiance* to be
neither prurient nor over-
academic. Exhibits were half-
hidden behind curvy gauze
screens to convey a sense of
enticement, secrecy, and the
forbidden. Nigel Coates's
initial sketch of the exhibition
(left) captures the sensual
intentions of the design.

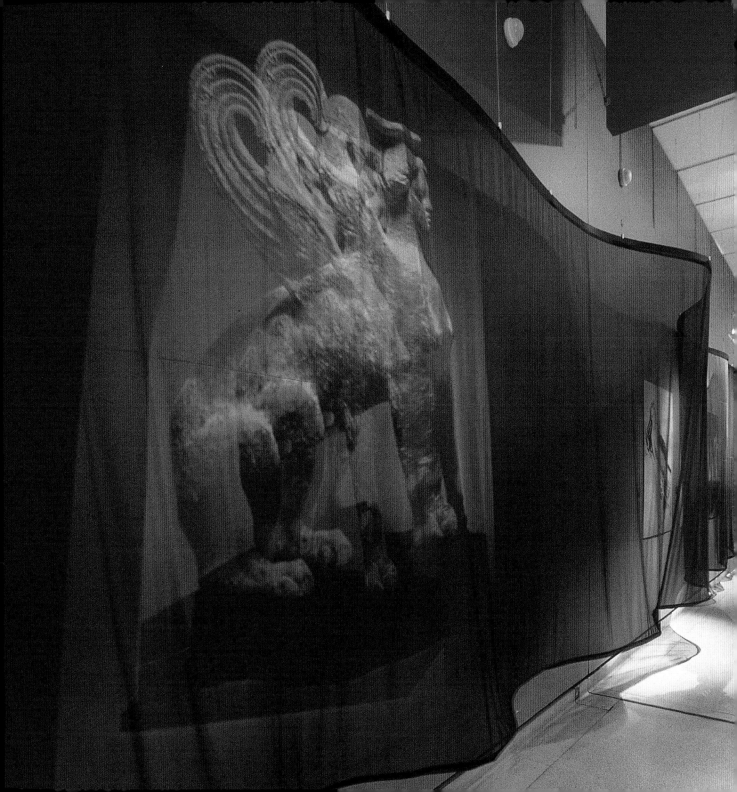

and forbidden spaces. The aim of the exhibition was to explore the impact that eroticism has had on design, recognizing that it can be just as much about seductiveness and desire as about form and function. Described as "an attempt to map out the erotic tradition of commercial art, fashion, advertising, and design from Mucha to Madonna," the exhibition looked at everything from Freud to fast cars. The various sections included an exploration of Art Nouveau, Surrealism, the 1960s sexual revolution, and sex in advertising. Coates's own designs—the Genie Stool, Legover Chair, and the Bridge City competition entry (see page 24)—were also featured alongside pieces and projects by other designers whose work has helped to shape the erotic landscape.

Orgasm into object: "Spiral to the Stars," proposal for the 1964 World's Fair in New York.

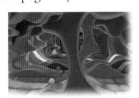

When the walls, floor, and ceiling all blend into one continuous sitting surface, as in Verner Panton's room at Visiona, our bodies can "enter" the furniture.

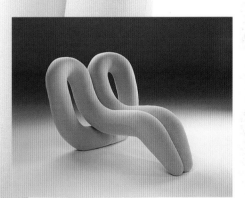

LEGOVER CHAIR
Partner & Co., 1997

The exhibition also included some of Coates's own designs. The Legover Chair continuously transforms itself—each of its three positions invites a different response.

THE POWER OF EROTIC DESIGN
Design Museum, London, 1997

Dimly lit and veiled by screens, exhibits included red mannequins wearing specially created costumes by Jean-Paul Gaultier (left) and Alexander McQueen (right). The introduction (inset) featured an outfit by Walter van Beirendonck.

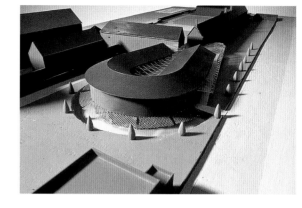

THE GEFFRYE MUSEUM has long been one of London's forgotten museums, the delightful home to a collection of old interiors, furniture, and decor originally gathered together by the former London County Council. The collection rests in a set of handsome Georgian almshouses founded by Sir Robert Geffrye, master of the Ironmongers' Company. The nearby Ironmongers' Baths continue to recall the altruistic nature of this City guild.

Two factors brought the Geffrye Museum out of its seclusion in 1998. The first was the sudden rise of its surrounding area, Shoreditch, for years a shabby and forlorn quarter of old industrial London but by the late 1990s a thriving community of artists, designers, architects, and young restaurateurs.

The horseshoe theater, and its partner the perspective stage, have been a long-standing model for a space that forms dynamic interaction.

The second factor was the opening of the museum's long-awaited extension, commissioned from Branson Coates. This had been a surprise decision, as one would have expected the task of extending this pretty museum to go to a firm of architects expert in conservation and with a proven knack of blending new buildings with existing fabric. The choice of BCA, however, has benefited both parties. The museum has not only raised its profile, but also acquired an extension that fuses a real sensitivity to site, and to the past, with an imaginative form and plan. The architects, meanwhile, have gained greatly from learning how to adapt their theatrical approach to both a context and a program that would require a gentle touch. There is no room for bombast or sheer theatricality here.

"It has the sort of fluid feel we intended," says Coates of the final result. "A floating glazed

The extension is entered via the museum's original Georgian almshouses— there is no façade as such.

coates'93

Topiary, with its clipped versions of twentieth-century domestic icons, was a way of keying together the spirits of the garden and the museum.

GEFFRYE MUSEUM EXTENSION
Model and sketch, 1998

Horseshoelike in plan, the extension leads off from the old building, only to return to it in one smooth movement around the central stairwell. The whole point of the new building is to make connections: between old and new, past and present, interior and exterior, popular taste and culture.

35

GEFFRYE
MUSEUM
EXTENSION
Plan and exterior view,
1998

**The extension takes the
form of a simple brick
horseshoe with pitched
slate roof and gable ends.
Despite the use of
traditional materials,
the overall impression
is light and airy.**

*(Right) Temple into volcano:
a staged event from the
heyday of Florentine drama.
(Below right) Spiral staircases
allow floors to literally flow
into one another.*

GEFFRYE
MUSEUM
EXTENSION
Interior view, 1998

**The café at the open end
of the horseshoe (below)
acts as a junction connecting
the old and new structures.
Downstairs, exterior
screens provide a protected
play-space for children
(bottom). A dragonlike
central stairwell (opposite)
leads up to the circulation
space on the upper
concourse (inset).**

roof joins the existing museum to the new brick horseshoe of the galleries, like a hand in a glove. We want it to set the stage for the more open attitude to space that underlies the design of the twentieth-century home." The new horseshoe of galleries can be reached only via the old almshouses. "The extension has no entrance of its own. Instead, visitors emerge from the old building into what is effectively a small covered piazza formed between the new galleries and the corner of the existing museum. This new space is deliberately exterior in spirit; the roof and walls are so light that to be in the restaurant here is the next best thing to being in the museum garden it overlooks. It's designed to be a breathing space between the old and new galleries."

With its horseshoe plan, the extension naturally encourages visitors to return to the old wing and toward the exit at the end of their visit. It is a remarkably gentle space, which makes imaginative use of traditional materials (handmade bricks, wood, slate) and yet is unexpected in its layout. What at first appears to be two brick sheds, with separate entrances from the restaurant piazza, turns out to be a single structure under a delicately ribbed glass roof. A generous central stairwell leads down to education rooms, galleries for temporary exhibitions and contemporary craft, storerooms, restrooms, and the garden. The new wing has also been designed to play a complex visual game with the densely packed and largely semi-industrial streetscape that exists beyond the calming walls of the collection itself. The Geffrye Museum has long been an oasis in a somewhat rough-and-ready district; the new extension adds a special magic, without bombast or rhetoric.

The Oyster House

THE OYSTER HOUSE was the surprise star at the 1998 *Ideal Home* exhibition in London. Sponsored by the *Daily Mail*, the exhibition—like that newspaper—has long been a bastion of Middle England taste and prejudices. But, in 1997, the exhibition organizers, together with the design and architecture magazine

A solid hovering above open ground, Le Corbusier's famous Villa Savoye at Poissy was a key starting point for our concept house.

Blueprint, devised a competition to design the "house of the future." Nigel Coates triumphed over 103 rival proposals with his Oyster House. The design was both a radical rethink of the dream country cottage or freestanding family home, and an expression of hip, urban loft living. It offered the privacy of the proverbial Englishman's castle, with the openness and free-form layout of a contemporary city apartment.

"It seemed an unlikely project for me," says Coates, "and yet every architect is fascinated by

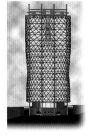

Gamma Tokyo brought together the entropic world of Japanese cities and the Oriental obsession with witty new products. Illustration for Brutus magazine.

the idea of designing the ideal family house. What I wanted to show was that it's possible to design a standard house type that could be built almost anywhere, in town or out of it. And then, just as importantly, to see if it was possible to balance communal and private space, to meet the needs of almost everyone who shares a house."

The budget was $165,000 U.S., and for this the house had to be fully furnished. The curvy, squashy, and otherwise voluptuous furniture, rugs, glassware, and vases were almost all designed by Coates. These were either sexy or playful or both; the sofas in particular had a bouncy castle-ish feel about them that made them

"Beirut," BCA's entry for a housing competition, took the form of a corseted luxury apartment building.

OYSTER HOUSE
Sketch and computer
rendering, 1998

The Englishman's castle
revisited: with its all-round
vistas, the symmetrical,
freestanding Oyster House
was designed to be
appropriate for urban,
suburban, and rural
settings. Its compasslike
form meant that its
orientation would capture
the best views of its site.

39

as popular with children as with adults. The furniture was designed for production and not simply to attract attention during the course of the *Ideal Home* show.

The symmetrically planned building is based around a pair of open stairs that cross each other at the center of the house, and act as structural bracing. Otherwise, the house is composed of a softwood lumber frame, capped with copper sheeting and, at ground-floor level, wrapped all around with Privalite glazing, a form of glass that can be made translucent or transparent at the touch of a switch. The upper floor has bird's-eye-like windows at each corner, giving the house its rather anthropomorphic or fairytale character. Inside, the Oyster House pays homage to the idea of easy modern living, a home to hang out and relax in, rather than a conventional, formally planned developer's brick box which, because of its rigid layout, dictates a certain way of life.

"The position of the stairs at the center of the house creates what is effectively a cruciform plan," says Coates. "It's much the same device that we used in the design of the Centre for Popular Music [see page 48] and in *powerhouse::uk* [see page 44]. It is a plan that offers you a sense of choice. As you come down the stairs from the private bedrooms, you can move into any corner

Sculptural forms from the 1960s: the futuristic world of Joe Colombo.

OYSTER HOUSE
Ideal Home Exhibition, 1998

Constructed in under one month, the Oyster House was a star attraction at the Ideal Home exhibition.

OYSTER LIGHTS
Prototype lighting, 1998

This multidirectional flat-pack lighting was designed to be scattered around the floor of the fictional teenage daughter's bedroom.

OYSTER DINING FURNITURE
Lloyd Loom, 1998

Squared simplicity brings out the sensuality of the Lloyd Loom traditional rolled paper weave.

Whether spaces or objects, everything Carlo Mollino touched seems to quote bodies as the source of dynamic flow.

of the house, without being forced by a rigid plan to go one way or the other. It's a nice, drifty kind of feeling that few houses allow. I also designed the curved floors as well as the easy furniture on the ground floor with the idea that those who are living here could feel free to just flop down anywhere and feel comfortable. This is a house to relax in."

The Oyster House certainly caught the popular imagination and might even have proved to house builders that a modern family home can be very different from the conventional neo-gothic and joke-oak piles that disfigure Britain from Penzance to Inverness.

GLASSWARE
Simon Moore, 1997

Most of the objects in the Oyster House were designed by Coates. The Retort Vases are part of a collection produced by Simon Moore.

OYSTER HOUSE
Living room and second-floor study, 1998

The living quarters are designed to be open, modern, and easy. The specially designed furniture and rugs are now available commercially (produced by Hitch Mylius and Kappa Lamda respectively). Crisscross stairs lead up to a flexible space that can be arranged to create a study, bedroom, bathroom, or whatever the concept home's occupants require.

THIS EXHIBITION REPRESENTED an extraordinary moment for contemporary architecture and design in Britain. Tony Blair's self-styled New Labour had just been voted into power at Westminster with a huge majority. Wanting his government to look youthful, thrusting, and dynamic, Blair was eager to make use of a radical new design to underline its new image. The media labeled this phenomenon (at least it was a phenomenon in Britain, where governments had always been famously style-free and ignorant of anything to do with architecture or design) "Cool Britannia." The name stuck, much to the prime minister's distress, and *powerhouse::uk* was widely seen as the quintessence of the "Cool Britannia" image.

Still from the opening of Ridley Scott's film Bladerunner, *a cityscape that seems to grow on its own and haunts the imagination.*

Whether the branding was right or wrong, this bouncy exhibition of "new" British design and creativity was highly successful. Originally designed as a showcase for the benefit of Far East delegates attending a Department of Trade and Industry-sponsored conference, *powerhouse::uk* was also opened to the public. It was housed in four silver-colored inflatable drums, the design and layout borrowed unashamedly from the practice's up-and-coming National Centre for Popular Music (see page 48). The drums were set down, memorably, in the great parade ground that stands facing London's St. James's Park and behind William Kent's wonderfully picturesque Horse Guards building. This site, used until then as a parking lot for civil servants, is overlooked by the bedrooms of the prime minister's official residence. The marriage of the silver drums with the picturesque skyline of Horse Guards and Whitehall was felicitous, the permanent and temporary buildings gaining in stature and delight from one another. The *powerhouse::uk* tents looked their best at dusk, when they were lit by a soft mauve or purple glow, which matched the thunderous evening clouds that hung over central London during the days of the exhibition.

The exhibition itself was divided into four themes, each occupying one of the four drums. The exhibitions were sassy and witty if not, perhaps, what the organizing officials would ideally have wanted. "The four

When taken out of context, the airport conveyor could liven up the gallery and take objects off their usual plinths.

POWERHOUSE::UK
Horse Guards Parade, London, 1998

The cruciform plan of the exhibition's central lobby (left) has become something of a Branson Coates trademark. The soft, temporary drums were set against the solid backdrop of the Horse Guards building (opposite).

Advertising on the back of buses means that giant images can float through the city at a larger-than-life scale, like a sort of silent animation.

spaces aimed to show how designers work in an interactive and interdisciplinary way," says Coates. "We wanted not merely to apply gloss to the product, but also to carry creativity to the user." It was this spirited atmosphere that made *powerhouse::uk* such an enjoyable event for so many people. Coates also used the exhibition as a forum for demonstrating how architecture has, for him, become one of the communicative arts. "We

incorporated examples of current architecture into a model landscape of cardboard towers and toy buses with massive ads. We aimed to show the side of architecture that wants to take part in the very stuff of communication that makes cities what they are." On a more practical level, the design of *powerhouse::uk* was also an interesting and useful exercise in observing how the National Centre for Popular Music might work day to day. It allowed Coates to get a feel of how one of the structures he had longed to create in central London might actually look, and whether it added to or subtracted from the existing spirit of the area.

POWERHOUSE::UK
Views of exhibition, 1998

While each of the four drums offered a distinctive spin on aspects of British creativity, they were all about making connections. Clockwise from top left: Creativity in Learning (schools, colleges, research); Creativity in Networking (new ways of working); Creativity in Communications (advertising, architecture, graphics, broadcast media); Creativity in Lifestyle (fashion, product design).

POWERHOUSE::UK
Design sketch, 1998

An early sketch for the Networking space; the idea was to house a whole family of computers, which would scoot around and talk to each other.

FOUR BIG STAINLESS-STEEL drums—a kind of giant drum set—house the new National Centre for Popular Music in Sheffield, England, due to open in 1999. This is Branson Coates's first major building and is as striking as expected. Sitting amid a spectacularly dreary part of this city of steel, it is surrounded by a dystopian townscape of the sort of brick buildings that have defaced most British cities over the past 25 years.

"The faceted surface of the drums has been designed to reflect the museum's surroundings in a kaleidoscopic and decidedly pop manner, making a virtue out of contextual necessity," says Coates. "Its percussive form and reflective surfaces mean that the Centre animates any number of views through Sheffield." The effect is a striking one, offering a kind of magical mystery tour of the city. At night the drums are designed to appear opaque; lit softly, they will reflect colored light rather than the broken images generated by the surrounding city.

The Centre provides a new visual backbeat to this industrial city, and one that you just can't lose. It is the hub of what is destined to become Sheffield's new quarter for "creative industry." "The idea of the drums was on one level a way of saying 'pop music'

I have something of an obsession with the centralized plan, as in Palladio's Villa Capra.

Despite their proximity, for functional reasons, industrial tanks create enigmatic spaces between each other.

NATIONAL CENTRE FOR POPULAR MUSIC
Sheffield, 1999

In keeping with the Centre's theme, the stainless-steel siding was unveiled by rappelling Elvises.

NATIONAL CENTRE FOR POPULAR MUSIC
Computer sketch

Giant drum set or "jukebox of pop experiences"? Despite its pop associations, Coates likens the NCPM's design to classical models, especially Palladio's Villa Capra near Vicenza.

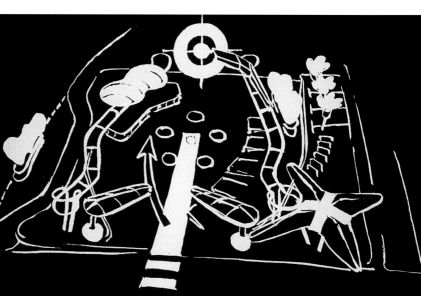

A scale model of the NCPM shows the four drums, their revolving roof vents, and the cruciform circulation space between them.

loud and clear," says Coates. It was also a very pragmatic way of dividing the Centre's four sections into four clear parts, and so allowing the visitors

to choose between them as they arrive in the cruciform lobby space that acts as the link between the drums. "Many museums force visitors along

Blast furnaces are at the heart of Sheffield's industrial heritage—their huge containers rival the scale of the buildings.

a particular route— you often find yourself tramping through galleries you have no interest in and just want to get through as quickly as possible. At Sheffield, you go in to the center of the building and then choose what you want to see."

The cruciform plan is reflected in the Oyster House (see page 38) and *powerhouse::uk* (see page 44). Coates describes it as "a device for amplifying the flux between concentric and eccentric space. There's both the discipline of the cross at the heart of the building, which projects up to the glazed roof, and the apparently unfathomable spaces of the drums that lead off it. It's this balance between discipline and a sense of adventure that will give the building something of the balance of pop music, which depends to a large extent on a steady beat overlaid with sounds that can lead you every which way."

Despite its dramatic form and finish, and the lack of conventional doors and windows, the Centre is a simple, logical space. It has demonstrated to critics of Branson Coates's polymorphous and sometimes perverse approach

Digital futures manifest themselves on the body. We wanted to transfer this sensibility to the city.

to architecture that there is real substance behind the practice's mellifluous rhetoric and braggadocio style.

NATIONAL CENTRE FOR POPULAR MUSI
Roof vent

The ingenious roof vents are designed to turn with the wind, lending the building a curiously kineti quality at the same time as providing natural low-energy ventilation.

50

A photographic collage reflects the fragmented, urban nature of the Centre. Collages such as this were made each week during construction to record the building's progress.

EXHIBITION
SPACE
Unrealized design, 1997

More than a collection of pop memorabilia, the Centre aims to give an insight into how pop music is made and performed. This unrealized design for one of the exhibition spaces is by Land Design Studio.

51

Body Zone

ON JANUARY 1, 2000, the first sight that will greet visitors to London's controversial Millennium Dome in Greenwich will be Branson Coates's giant Body. This sculpture of intertwined male and female figures is a building and an exhibition pavilion

Two bodies in harmony: Etruscan tomb in the Villa Giulia, Rome.

in its own right. Unsurprisingly, the theme is the working of the human body and the state of our current understanding of it. Given the inauspicious start to the "Body Zone" project, Coates performed a minor miracle to turn the initial, much-maligned proposals into a design of great power and even beauty.

Coates has long been fascinated with the idea of how the human body relates to the design and workings of the city. "The city is an organism," he says, "a giant body if you like. It has head, hands, heart, and every other organ. It lives and breathes." He was an obvious candidate for the ambitious Body project. "It was a fascinating challenge to reverse the respective scales of the body and the city. The Body Zone is a kind of cityscape in its own right, a giant model of a man and woman, which real live humans can walk through and around. It's the body seen and experienced on the scale of an urban monument."

The earliest proposal for the Body, which was shown to a skeptical and bemused media, was for a giant seated hermaphrodite stretching out to greet a baby of equally indeterminate sex. This

Giant body parts contrast with real, live humans and the imposing architectural backdrop of the Hermitage Museum in St. Petersburg, Russia.

image had nothing to do with Branson Coates, who had yet to be invited to join the New Millennium Experience team. The proposal met with a storm of derision in the media. Why a hermaphrodite? Would the baby have to wear a giant diaper? Unhelpful and even

BODY ZONE
Conceptual collage

"We wanted to imbue the Body with feeling and emotion, which is why we chose two figures in a soft embrace rather than one standing heroically upright," says Coates. Initial explorations were primarily made using 3-D models, but it was this collage which crystallized the idea of intertwined male and female forms.

Site for the Body: the Millennium Dome, Greenwich, under construction in late 1998. The plan shows the Dome's 14 exhibition zones; Body Zone is number 14.

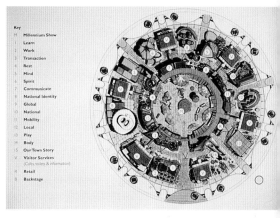

Key
M Millennium Show
1 Learn
2 Work
3 Transaction
4 Rest
5 Mind
6 Spirit
7 Communicate
8 National Identity
9 Global
10 National
11 Mobility
12 Local
13 Play
14 Body
Our Town Story
V Visitor Services
(Cafes, toilets & information)
R Retail
B Backstage

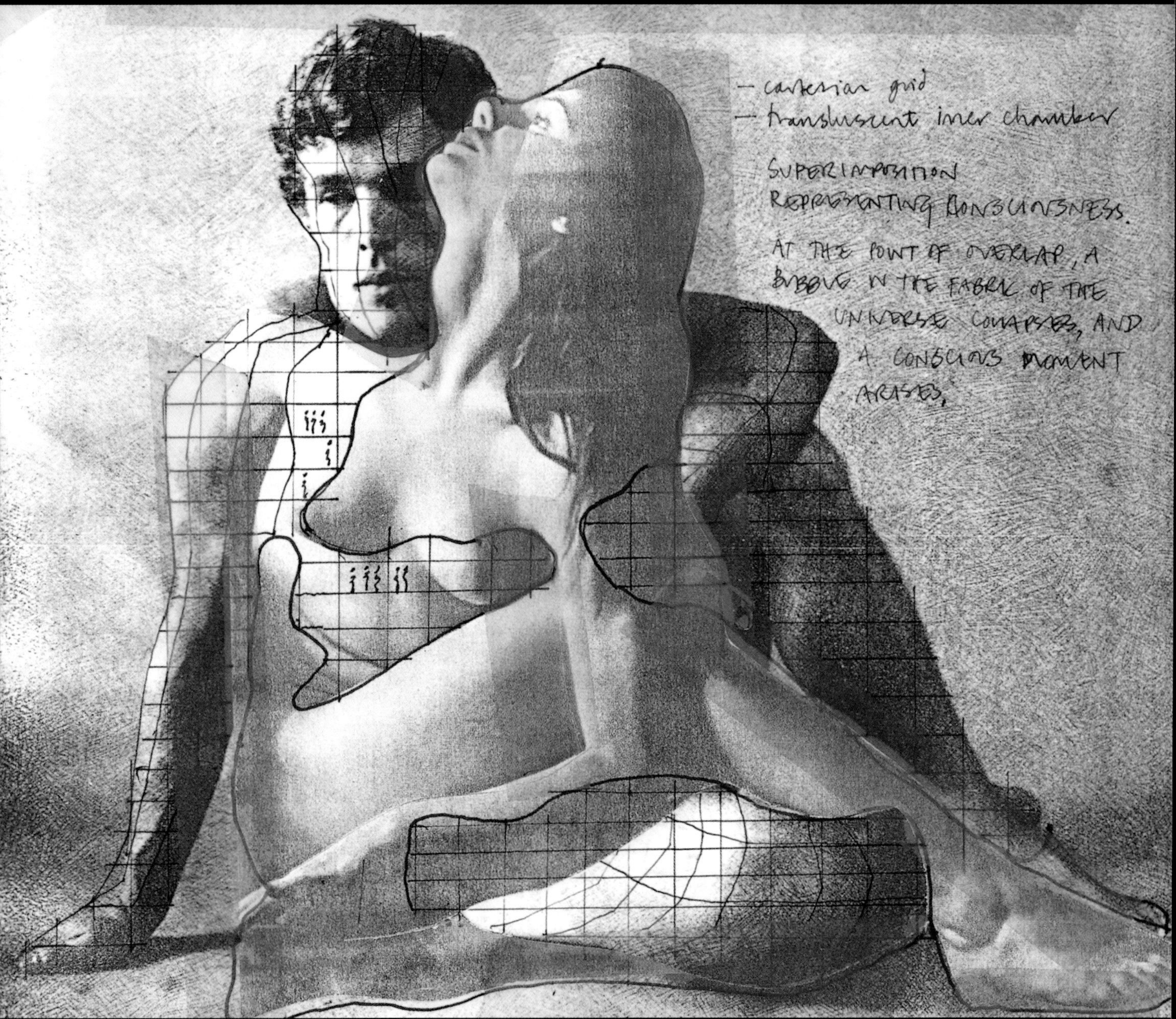

- cartesian grid
- translucent inner chamber

SUPERIMPOSITION
REPRESENTING CONSCIOUSNESS.

AT THE POINT OF OVERLAP, A
BUBBLE IN THE FABRIC OF THE
UNIVERSE COLLAPSES, AND
A CONSCIOUS MOMENT
ARISES.

53

BODY ZONE
Notebook sketch, 1998

Part of the initial brief was
for visitors to enter via a
"landscape," and then
choose their own points of
interest. Coates wanted to
achieve a sense of flow and
continuity from landscape
to figure and back again.
Although the landscape
idea was subsequently
dropped, in this sketch the
Body itself is close to its
final form.

La Specola:
The Body
Acker...
Kostur
Sherman
talk: Iwona

how none of us are normal.
to try others bodies
to endure, and transgress pain.

BODY ZONE
Annotated sketch, 1998

Coates wanted to avoid the Body becoming a giant sculpture, admired for its appealing form alone. Layers of activity and meaning were added in order to increase its resonance and avoid overt realism. A neon aura between the two figures represents energy, while a necklace of scrolling messages signifies collaboration. One foot takes an aeronautical shape and is lifted dynamically in the air, while the other remains grounded in its surroundings. The life-sized body in the hand-held sphere represents destiny.

"He-Man, She-Woman"—shop mannequins designed by Nigel Coates in 1988.

cruel comparisons were made between the ambition for the Body and the pathologically exaggerated golden statue of Nero in Rome, which the emperor commissioned for the site where the Colosseum stands today, and a giant figure showing the workings of the human body made for an exhibition in Nazi Germany.

The hermaphrodite and crawling baby soon disappeared. "We wanted to celebrate the male and female figures," says Coates, "to recognize the newly established equality between the sexes and yet to emphasize their differences, too—all in one giant figure. The answer, we felt, wasn't one sexless torso, but a single structure that embraced both

Bodies in detail: Nigel Coates's "No Furs" stand at the Habitat and Identita exhibition, Arezzo, Italy, 1990.

Taking stock of Le Corbusier's "Modulor" man.

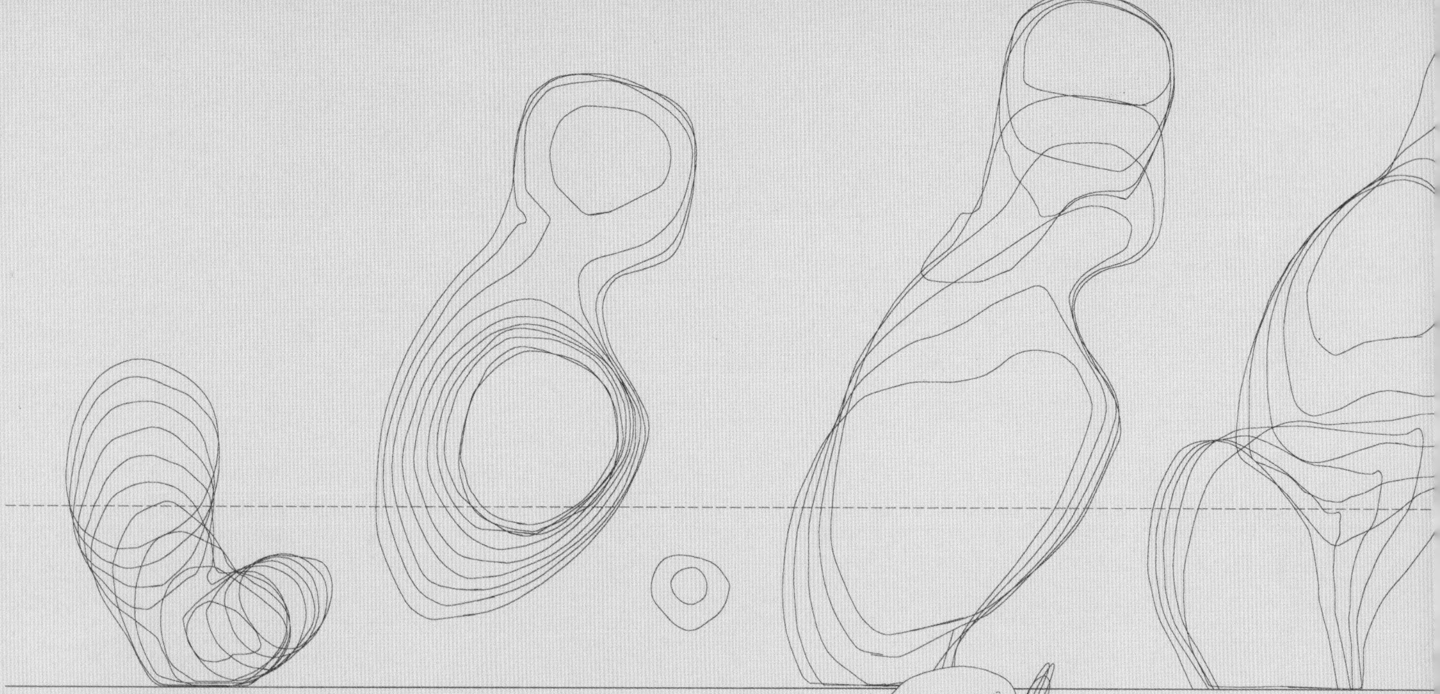

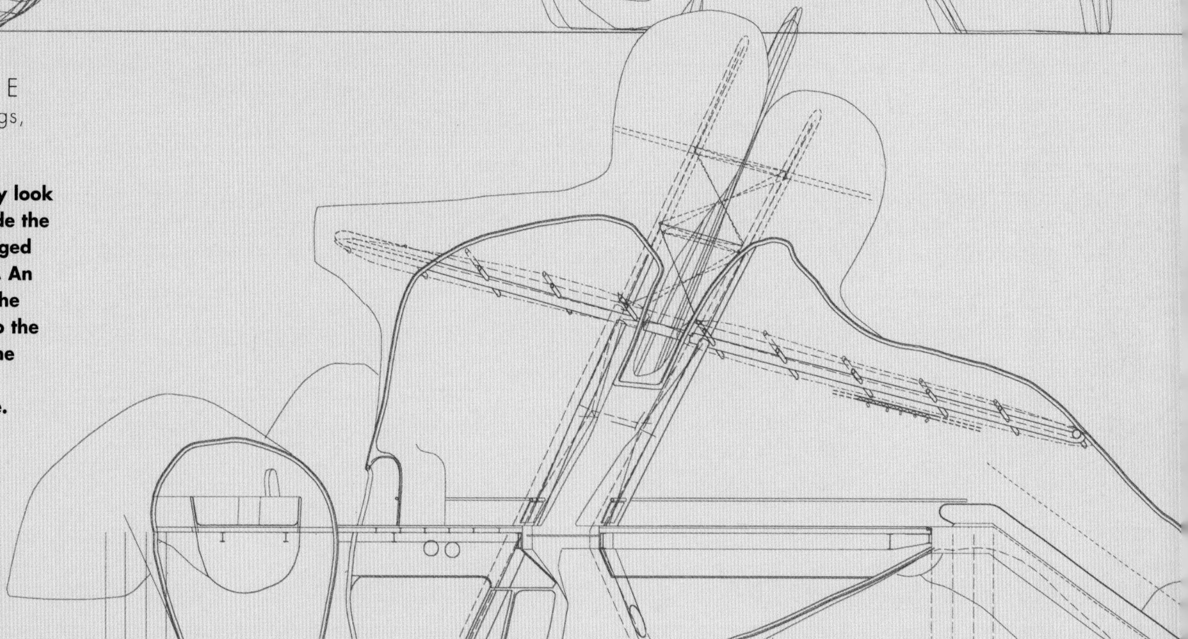

BODY ZONE
Computer drawings,
1998

The outer form may look sculptural, but inside the Body is a fully fledged exhibition pavilion. An escalator through the "male" leg leads to the main platform of the two-story walk-through experience.

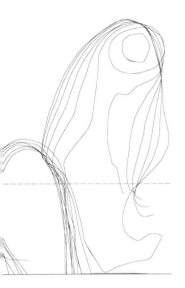

Body as construction: statue at Hyde Park Corner in London enmeshed in scaffolding and gauze.

A Michelangelo slave adds sensuality to this table by Carlo Mollino.

the male and the female form. It was a difficult thing to do, not least because of what it might say or symbolize to people; the structure also had to act as a complex exhibition pavilion telling the story of the human body."

The final version of Branson Coates's giant Body is derived in part from a beautiful and very moving Etruscan funerary monument of a smiling husband with his arm around his wife. (The monument is one of the star exhibits in the Villa

Giulia Museum in Rome.) In the case of the huge 88-foot (27-meter) high Body, all details—fingers, genitalia, individual features—have been spirited away. What is left is a sculptural form that is remarkably restrained for Branson Coates, and yet at the same time is capable of housing a major exhibition. The scale of the Body is heroic: it is designed to rise up to the apex of the Dome, and real humans will look like ants crawling across it.

Because the Body is an exhibition pavilion and not an artwork in the accepted sense, Coates has worked to animate the design and almost willfully to undermine its near purity of form. Although the earliest models were somewhat reminiscent of Barbara Hepworth sculptures, in its final guise the Body will have anything but a

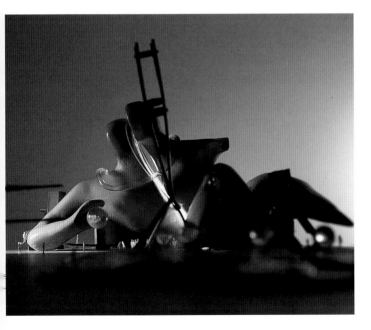

BODY ZONE
Scale model, 1998

The reclining figures, says Coates, are designed to "lean towards the visitors in a friendly way"—all the more necessary because of the Body's monumental scale.

57

smooth skin, its surface being lit and otherwise enervated by exposed visitor platforms, ramps, and other devices. "We want to contradict its status as sculpture," says Coates. "We want the Body to be tactile, but not in the sense of a sculpture destined for an art gallery."

Inside, the Body frames two major exhibition floors, each 60 feet (18 meters) apart and linked by elevators and an escalator. Following a predefined route, visitors will climb through one of the legs and emerge from the side of the "male" half of the body, at the point where his arm reaches around the female side; they will then walk along a ramp, giving high views of the Millennium Experience, before entering the female zone. The two halves of the Body will become one inside: "they flow into one another harmoniously," says Coates. In the great scheme of things, surely this is the ideal relationship, whether architecturally or between the sexes.

BODY ZONE
Computer simulation,
1998

The Body is the first thing that visitors to the Millennium Experience will see. Coates views it as a kind of cityscape in its own right—the body seen and experienced on the scale of an urban monument.

*City as body…
body as city. Ecstacity
comes full circle.*

58

59

1949
Nigel Coates born in Malvern, Worcestershire.

1971–74
Studies architecture at Nottingham University.

1974–77
Continues architectural studies at the Architectural Association (AA), London.

1978–86
Teaches at the AA. In 1983 forms NATO (Narrative Architecture Today) group with some of his students. Holds one-man exhibition, ArkAlbion, at the AA in 1984.

1985
Forms the Branson Coates partnership with Doug Branson. Begins working on a number of club and bar projects in Japan.

1986
Opening of Caffè Bongo and Bohemia Jazz Club, Tokyo. Interior design for Jasper Conran Shop, London.

1988
Designs Jigsaw shops for London (Kensington) and Bristol, and Katharine Hamnett shops for London (Sloane Street) and Glasgow. Opening of the Arca di Noè restaurant building in Sapporo, Japan.

1989
Opening of Hotel Marittimo, Otaru, Japan. Designs Jasper Conran shop, Tokyo, and Situationists exhibition for the Centre Georges Pompidou, Paris.

1990
Opening of the Nishi Azabu Wall, a commercial building in Tokyo. Designs Jigsaw shop for King's Road (London), and Katharine Hamnett/Hamnett Active shops, Tokyo.

1991
Opening of Taxim restaurant, bar, and nightclub, Istanbul. Designs Jigsaw shop for Brompton Road, London.

1992
Designs Jigsaw shop for St. Christopher's Place, London. Wins invited competition to design the new gallery extension for the Geffrye Museum, London. *Ecstacity* exhibition shown at the AA, London, and at the Fondation pour l'Architecture, Brussels.

1993
Opening of La Forêt and Nautilus restaurants, Schiphol Airport, Amsterdam. Designs interiors, perfume department, and bookstore/café for Liberty Regent Street, London, and Liberty Tax Free shop for Heathrow Airport, Terminal 3.

1994

Designs further Jigsaw shops for London, Dublin, Manchester, Glasgow, and Tokyo; designs Fashion Concept Room and Kurt Geiger shoe department at Liberty Regent Street, London.

1995

Designs further Jigsaw shops for London and Tokyo, and Liberty shops for Stratford-upon-Avon, London (Fenchurch Street), and Heathrow. Wins competition to design the National Centre for Popular Music in Sheffield. Appointed professor of Architectural Design at the Royal College of Art, London.

1996

Designs *Living Bridges* exhibition at the Royal Academy, London. Participates in Thames Water Habitable Bridge competition and *Financial Times* Millennium Bridge competition. Opening of Bargo bar, Glasgow. Launch of Coates for Simon Moore glass vase collection.

1997

Designs *The Power of Erotic Design* exhibition, Design Museum, London, and *Look Inside!*, British Council touring exhibition. Wins competition for Midland Arts Centre development, Birmingham. Wins *Blueprint* magazine's Concept House competition to design a speculative subdivision house; wins competition to design *powerhouse::uk* exhibition, London.

1998

Opening of *powerhouse::uk* exhibition. Oyster House shown at the *Ideal Home* Exhibition, London. Opening of the Geffrye Museum extension, London, and Moshi Moshi Sushi restaurant, Canary Wharf, London. Exhibition and interior design of British pavilion for Expo 98, Lisbon. Launch of rugs for Kappa Lambda, OXO chairs for Hitch Mylius, and Oyster Dining Furniture for Lloyd Loom.

1999

Opening of the National Centre for Popular Music, Sheffield. Ongoing work includes: British pavilion for Expo 2000, Hanover; Shakespearean Theater, Gdansk, Poland (redevelopment of a seventeenth-century theater); refurbishment of Christie's auctioneers, London; Body Zone for Millennium Dome, Greenwich, London.

Index

Acknowledgments

The publishers wish to thank Nigel Coates, Gerrard O'Carroll and all at Branson Coates Architecture for their kind assistance with all aspects of this book.

Picture credits

Every effort has been made to trace all copyright holders and obtain permissions.

The editor and publisher sincerely apologise for any inadvertent errors or omissions.

Allan Bell/BCA: page 6.

Allan Bell/Raj Chaudhary: pages 50/51 top.

Valerie Bennett: pages 10 left, 28 middle left.

Blueprint (1992): page 17.

Branson Coates Architecture: pages 16 right, 20 top right and bottom, 21, 22/23 middle and bottom, 23 top, 34 bottom, 36 top left (plan), 38 bottom, 39 right, 46 bottom, 48 bottom, 49 inset, 53, 55 middle right, 55 bottom, 56, 61 bottom middle (bridges).

Bridgeman Art Library, London/New York (photograph Bernard Cox): page 52 top (JB 54679; COX 1A Sposi Sarcophagus, in the Villa Giulia, Rome; Etruscan, 6th century BC).

Richard Bryant/Arcaid: page 60 bottom right.

Nigel Coates: pages 5, 16 left, 20 top left, 23 right, 24 top left, 30 top and right, 35 left, 38 top and middle, 38/9 background, 40 bottom, 42 background, 45, 46 top, 48 top and bottom right, 50 middle left, 54, 55 top left and background, 57 top, 58 left, 60 left.

Nigel Coates/BCA: pages 9 middle, 10 right, 13, 14 bottom, 15.

Nigel Coates/Stewart Helm: pages 12 left, 60 bottom middle and top right.

Simon Eager: page 54 top.

Andreas Feininger: pages 26 bottom left, 48 bottom left.

C. Filioux and J.H. Yum: page 28 left.

Peter Fleissig: page 12 right.

Graham Gaunt: pages 50 bottom right, 61 far right.

Edward Valentine-Hames: pages 8 left, middle right and right, 9 left and right, 11 left, 18, 19 left, 60 bottom left.

Hayes Davidson (illustration): page 59

©Image Bank: pages 35 right, 50 top.

David LaChapelle: page 28 top left.

Land Design Studios: page 51 bottom.

Carlo Mollino Archives, Turin: pages 30 bottom, 42 top, 57 bottom.

Simon Moore, London, Ltd (photographs Philip Vile): pages 12 left, 42 right, 61 bottom left.

NMEC: page 52 bottom right

Erik Oesterlund: pages 24 middle and bottom, 25.

Verner Panton, Basle: page 33 bottom left.

Partner & Co.: page 32 right.

Josh Pullman: page 19 bottom.

Andrew Putler: page 49 main picture.

QA Photos/NMEC: page 52 top right

Guy Ryecart: page 57 bottom.

Phil Sayer: pages 26 right, 27, 28 top right, middle right and bottom right, 29 right, 31, 32, 47 top right, 60 near right (Moshi Moshi restaurant).

Snowdon: page 14 left.

©Stock Market: page 44 middle.

Thomas Struth: page 22 left.

Christine Sullivan: page 61 top middle.

Philip Vile: pages 36 top left (exterior), middle and bottom, 37, 41, 42 left, 43, 47 top left and bottom.

V'soske Joyce: page 11 right.

Paul Warchol: page 8 middle left.

©Warner Brothers: page 44 top.

Stephen White: pages 11 middle, 34 top, 61 middle left.

Tom Whitehead: page 44 bottom.

F.R. Yerbury/Architectural Association: page 36 middle right (Melk Abbey staircase).